PROTECTED
for a
PURPOSE

Lalita Walker

ISBN 978-1-0980-4273-8 (paperback)
ISBN 978-1-0980-4274-5 (hardcover)
ISBN 978-1-0980-4275-2 (digital)

Christian Faith Publishing, Inc.
832 Park Avenue
Meadville, PA 16335
www.christianfaithpublishing.com

Printed in the United States of America

CONTENTS

ACKNOWLEDGMENTS

To Our Heavenly Father full of grace and mercy:
    I honor you with this book *Protected for a Purpose*.
Thank you for being the source of my life.
Making all things possible for those who believe.
I would also like to extend my appreciation and gratitude to:
Nora Tatina, Deja Wimms, and Michael Bedell for wisdom and guidance.

Then finally to my family and friends, a special thanks for much love and support.

1

Protected for a Purpose

I was a child that had few or little words to say at around four years of age. I hid the issues of my heart. God says to "keep thy heart with all diligence; For out of it are the issues of life" (Prov. 4:23 KJV). As I think about this, the heart holds, carries, and circulates. I believe that what you think about or meditate on sets in your heart becomes your reality. It can also determine your purpose. I was so concerned about my appearance that I caused self-affliction (suffering on oneself, anything that burdens the spirit, ill treatment, pressure, pain, distress) For example, a wrong emotion, suffer hardship, when used in the present experience of believers refers almost invariably to that which comes on them without. In my mind, there was a constant replay of negativity of myself. (You're not cute, disliked, not adding up to others' abilities, comprehension, and smarts.)

It contained my mind with trouble thoughts, and I was hurting myself with myself, looking for whatever people said is wrong with me and then coming into agreement with it. I wanted to change myself as far as appearance to accommodate others, accepting all the negativity spoken and allowing that to eat at my soul. Instead of focusing on what's right how to please the Lord Jesus Christ. For example, a server, helping people. I allowed words of others to justify who I am, not knowing at this time that words have power. That you are who you say you are, no matter what. Because I focused so much time, thoughts, and energy on other people in the wrong way (giving them authority with their words over me), this opened the door for distruction. "Death and life are in the power of the tongue. And they that love it shall eat the fruit there of" (Prov. 18:21).

As a child, I monitored people's personality, expressions, and actions toward me. I had tight curly hair with a gap between my teeth that caused a lot of looks and stares. Some even frowned and laughed, but I maintain without conflict. In my own family, some were ashamed of me. I stayed clear from them occasionally in public. I was told, "We'll bring you something back." Other kids in the family that had a different appearance could go. My family was a big melting pot, with all kinds of colors and backgrounds. I watched those adults embrace one ethnicity and not the other. They favored only those who were like their appearance. There were many secrets in my family that separated us. For example, who said this, or who did that. I recall no family reunions for my immediate family growing up. Even though defrauded out of the best relationship of their life. When you think about it, sometimes, the person was innocent you thought differently about and words said inappropriately out of anger caused division; someone else was controlling the situation. It's unfortunate that lost time can come to pride.

As I look at this, how some had better jobs and opportunities and selected those in the family to help. Even when relatives died in the family, money and property neglected, those in charge of the money cared only for their immediate family. The other family members made a way for themselves. This put the match on the fire! It's amazing how communication in relationships is so important. It helps to keep the unity no matter the age group. Just learning from other people's perspectives and views can cause one to have a better understanding of the other and sometimes compassion. I wasn't comfortable around some of my family members because the tension was high. My feelings and emotions were running wild, I caused myself low self-esteem.

It is written, "For we dare not make ourselves of the number or compare ourselves with some that commend themselves. But they measuring themselves by themselves and comparing themselves among themselves, are not wise" (2 Cor. 10:12 KJV). This taught me that even as a child, I was in people's perspective whether right or wrong. The belief given to me whether good or bad is how I perceived myself. Whatever they said to me, this is who I became. It's like slapping with a tag and branded. I believed those family members had it all together, there was a comparison between myself and them. But later on, life happens, and some had no control over obstacles and tribulations. This caused much suffering.

Those relatives watched while I come to the door. It was closed in my face, and not open unless grandma was there. I put my head down and walked away, thinking about what I did wrong to separate. In their surroundings issues on my hair or clothes became the topic. The style I portrayed was different for a child. I loved dresses and sundresses everywhere I go, and my hair maintained in a upward ponytail. I resembled no one else. It's sad to say I had no relationship or bond with those family members. They treated me like an outsider. There's no understanding what I sustained from family. I was a kid looking for love. Our Father God teaches us that:

> Love is patient, love is kind. It does not envy, it does not boast, it is not proud. It does not dishonor others, it is not self-seeking, it is not easily angered, it keeps no record of wrongs. Love does not delight in evil but rejoices with the truth. It always protects always trusts, always hope, always perseveres. (1 Cor. 13:4–7 NIV)

My heart loved them unreasonably, but there was a disconnection. I believed a productive family that works together is a powerful union. Family members can open doors for advancement, growth, and opportunites for everyone, even in life. For example, someone in the family could help you with ideas, business, jobs, health, relationships, or wealth, etc. If there were better relationships in the beginning, including structure, moral, values and a foundation, this would manifest in you. It would help relationships outside the house. Just learning how to communicate with each other. Connecting, understanding, listening, and respecting one another and most important, love. This can maintain throughout our day, as we interact with people. Love is God's foundation, his nature, creation. Love can look past the outside and see the heart, knowing that God loves all the same. "Train up a child in the way he should go: and when he is old; he will not depart from it" (Prov. 22:6 KJV).

The beauty of God, for we are all made in the image of God. A workmanship, the Potter and the clay. Love is a part of me. I couldn't change it or stop it. Those could walk away from family with no problem, but I still desired a wonderful family, knowing that the union is abundant. You can be in a place where you're going through but unaware. I was not in control of my life, but thank God Almighty for a ram in a bush. As if she knew my heart and feelings. My great-grandma came and embraced me with a big hug, picked me up. She would always squeeze and smash you so tight; your legs would just swing. Grandma carried me to her room. We laid down and watched different ministers on television (Jimmy Swaggart and Jim Bakker). At this moment the word of God revealed to me, and I'm protected for a purpose.

At home, my mom worked a lot, sometimes mornings and nights. We had different babysitters. My mom was unaware of the abuse. My heart was full of hurt. Being rejected. For example, being dismissed in a relationship, forsaken or casted off, and it feels horrible. I needed help. In grammar school, my mother would always protect us. If there was a conflict at school, she's coming to rectify the problem. Nothing happens to her kids, and she's there. You could see she cared for us, but I was uncomfortable talking to her, so I didn't; I stayed "bottly" up with myself. My mom slept long hours. When she got up, we were already asleep, missing her a lot of days. There's no doubt, we never hungered for a meal. They were hot and homemade by her and others. A full course meal with desserts. My mom made cakes from scratch; my favorite pound cake and caramel cake, she also made homemade ice cream. On our way to school, they prepared lunch for us. We always had our favorite lunch box ready to go and packed. She made a lot of our clothes, when time permitted by purchasing patterns and materials. I don't know when she had time to do this, but it happened.

I would watch her lay that pattern out, pin it together with the material, and make a shape or a design. The design would be the same as the pattern. Then she sewed the material together, and they were the best clothes. That no one matched or resembled us. We were unique in our own way. My mother provided the best of her abilities. Even when sick, she made it better whether her or us. For provisions, she had to leave us with others. These were only the beginning of my troubles. I stayed quiet about people, I went to my room and sat on the floor in the closet quietly. When times were getting the best of me, I needed to go away. The closet was a meditation place for me. My thoughts were not racing. My mind was clear and not scrambled. I am calm and at peace. Feeling the air blowing across my body as if it stripped me.

Another place I would go was under the bed on the floor. The floor was my security blanket. I felt safe. No one can hurt me. I laid out facedown and slept, I would even roll up like a baby. My sleep was so deep! "He that dwelleth in the secret place of the most high shall abide under the shadow of the Almighty" (Ps. 91:1 KJV). For God is my safety and my protection. Going to the closet or under the bed was not the plan but it happened. I gave it no thought. This was new to me as well. I believe I found my secret place at a young age. Even I experienced loneliness, played by myself with toys or a doll. I had no other choice, only a few asked, could I come over. The other kids would leave with siblings, friends, or relatives that had their picks. I learned to adapt with situations.

Then one day, I dreamt of a green forest with rays of white thin lights going in different directions, like spotlights before a movie presentation. I was walking down a path through the forest when I saw a baby on the grass. This baby was lying on the grass under a big tree that had many leaves on it. As I walked toward the baby, I saw no one. The child was full of light and was left there abandoned. But there was not a sound coming from the child, no crying and no tears. This baby was pure white of another kind, dazzling like snow. The child was wrapped in a white blanket and dressed in a white baptism gown with no hair. I picked up the baby, very energetic, full of life, and much movement. There was eye-to-eye contact from this

11

child—so attentive and alert. I held the child tight over my shoulders, as if I knew what to do. Carrying this baby like a mother and only a child myself. This might sound strange, but I walked tall and strong as if someone was walking me. My back looked wide and solid, like another form was present. It's amazing no one touched me or attacked me. There's something's hiding not visible to the eye. I walked freely with no fear, not knowing what's ahead of me. I made it out.

Then another night, I dreamt that someone or something was after me. I saw no image or person, but I heard a movement perhaps at a pace. Trying to harass me and getting closer. My hearing is keen and maybe sharp. Whatever's out there, displease and angry is unknown. It wanted something from me, I suspect the child. To reconsider what I did and give the child back. I did not comply, this was beyond reasoning. The truth of the matter is, this child was a baby, not an animal in the forest. Is there any wrong in saving a child? *What's coming for me?* I thought. I feel the need to protect the child and hold on. This shadow was fierce with horror and terror to consume me. I couldn't see myself anymore, but my feelings and emotions were alive. I jumped straight up out the dream in a wreck shaken by what's happening.

I was in my bed, an object came straight and long at my head with the mouth open. I began screaming from the depth of my soul with agony and pain hollering, "Turn on the lights." No one came to turn on the lights, no time soon. I was afraid then. These dreams seem so real or alive. That this was unbelieveable. Then one day, the dream appeared in my mom's house. I woke up in the natural, got out the bed, and left my bedroom. Then walked in the living room and right before my eyes, a forest again, not the same as the first. Nor green or bright, but foggy. The trees were basically naked with little to no leaves. This reminds me of an aftermath from a forest fire. You could tell destruction was there.

It was darker, almost a replica of the first. This time, I could see the faces of people and images. The look was of suffering and despair, as if those were mentally incapacity with their minds. Their focus was intimidating, the eye contact was strong. Waiting for you to intervene and stop the chaos. There were no words spoken, but it seemed so real. I thought of a movie projector played before you through a lens. One after the other, I saw people through our house jumping at you. In a place of captivity with no direction and a creepy situation. Then I saw a group of people near to each other standing wanting to be free. It was so real. I was racing and fighting for a way out, not knowing which way to turn. Then loosen from this night-mare with no remembrance until now. Fear consumed me at a young age. (It seems best to understand it as caused by the intimidation of adversaries.)

Signs of fear—anxiety, dread, worry, an uneasiness in the mind (fear of trouble, fear of death, fear of sickness, fear of failure). "For God hath not given us the spirit of fear; but of power and of love and of a sound mind" (2 Tim. 1:7 KJV). I woke up in the natural, in a sweat, not understanding what I saw. I didn't talk or say a word, keeping quiet was my best option. This definitely is out of control and unbearable for a child. Why me? Later on, when I watched tele-vision, or something hurtful happened, I saw it in a dream which appeared in the natural. How could this be? A constant attack every night for a while. There was a battle in my mind. It was only God who saved me from being displaced as a child.

Another example, the television show *Roots* was so traumatiz-ing. At my grandmother's house, this show was on a lot, series after series. Out of respect, no one touches her television. I had to watch the program. It played over and over in my mind, the abuse, beatings and lynchings. When I went to sleep, my mind was in agony. I woke up screaming and crying as usual. When I walked through the house, someone was hanging from the door post with a leash around the neck; then other times hanging from a tree. I saw this many times in our home, there's no words to describe it. These were terrible times. No one asked me about my dreams, and I was in distress. The secret place was my only answer, and I sat for long periods of time. I could breathe and be safe, wanting to be still and quiet. I was a peculiar child but a fighter.

Listening to music would also help me free my mind, but love songs caused much tears. It might sound strange, but I cried over

"We Are the World." This song would touch my heart. As I listen to each artist, I could feel hurt, sorry, and pain through the song. Their voices shook me. The words penetrated in my soul. A message for help and love anywhere you can. Reach out to people, hug someone, tell them you love them, and give them a kiss. There are many people lacking in this area. In some cases, "I love you" is never said. The more I heard it, the more I cried. It was not a regular cry. But my heart aching. After I cried, there was a release; whatever was on my mind, it's gone. I felt better, there's noting stopping my progress. I've heard people say, "Cry and get it all out," as crying cleanses the soul. At this point in my life, I understand this. As time continued on, I struggled at bedtime. Wanting the lights to stay on. I heard sleep, and I screamed. Then I received attention from my mother.

I understand that someone or something was attacking me constantly. But mom never knew. How could I explain the way I feel? I was bad to some and this was the outcome. I disagree with this accusation who knows me but God Almighty. I was afraid to turn off the lights for many years. What happens if I close my eyes, where will I be or who will I see? Fear wanted my peace and control my life. It's real. To hinder my mind and stop any advancement in the future. I worried and kept with fear; it's a trap for me taken with no warning, but I still went to sleep anyway in the dark and cried continuedly. Then one day, my mom took us to church, out of the blue. It became mandatory, no exception in our family. We learned that my mom went to church as a child, and it's beneficial to study the Gospel and come together in unity. I had to be within reach, to save my soul.

There was one relative who was an inspiration to us all. She went to church faithfully. She cooked, cleaned, and served on different auxiliaries—finance and choir—and she paid tithes consistently. Blessings followed her throughout her life. Attending church was a privilege, and I loved it. My family sang in the choir at church, but somewhere, I changed. I saw different families together; those who kissed and showed love. They cared about each other and showed much compassion. I was outside looking in. A feeling of depression came over me. My family showed no compassion or love in this way. We never talked at the table as a family or shared our concerns.

There was a hole in my heart (depression, no excitement at times, sad demeanor, not wanting to eat, stay in a particular place). "Create in me a clean heart, O God; and renew a right spirit within me" (Ps. 51:10 KJV).

I had a look of sadness, not much activity to the point of depression. In my room a lot with no company. Who would spend time with me? I remained forgotten and lonely. When I went outside, some were better to me than my own. Then one day, I went directly around the corner to a friend's house. No one knew I left and who really cares. The side door was open, I stood there patiently waiting. Our girlfriend's brother took me without hesitation. Which was unexpected. He was always nice to me. We went to the store. He bought candy, chips, or ice cream. We walked down the street like father and daughter. I thought he was a friendly person. At the house, we went to the bedroom. No one called to address my dissappearance. He took me right to bed. The brother held me with one leg over my body while laying next to me. He pretended to take a nap.

I didn't see or hear anyone in the house, no one knew I was there. This guy was sneaking to do things. I remember him touching me to arouse himself. The look was of pure lust. An attraction for kids. He was admiring my body I had no idea. This guy was putting himself in a position to engage. This may sound strange, I felt nothing. There was a mask over my face and a cover over my body. An adult performance of sexual acts taking place before my eyes. The body had no movement. Dead with no life in it, and he was unaware. No concern if I cried or not. There were no feelings or emotions. The inner part of me was not present. I didn't scream. Somehow I dissappeared, taken and removed without recognition, or perhaps your body can be in one place and you in another watching—the spirit part of you.

The body appeared to be a robot form. It looks real, but deceiving. There were no signs of activity on my clothes. When I came home, I told no one. I continued to be troubled. Then bitterness was all over me (of a condition of extreme hostility, poignant grief, and hatred). Signs: Unforgiveness, jealous, irritated (Example of bitterness: Due to life challenges or past decisions). I'm disgusted with this. Nothing had much meaning to me then. I was in no compliance with the situation. I kept isolating myself. But then one day, I looked up. My mom bought a cat. Kitty was my best friend. He was basically winter white with red pink eyes that shined in the dark. He made me smile. I carried him like a baby. Hugged him, talked to him, and squeezed him. I would sing love songs to kitty. Then other times, I would listen to R&B music and shake kitty's body like a rubber band and dance him around and laugh.

He watched me at night while I slept, lying on his side like a lion swinging his tail from both sides. Kitty responded if you spoke. It's impossible to sneak in the room without him seeing you. I could talk to him about anything. If there's no food Kitty still followed expecting. I loved him; my days were great until difficulties arose at school. I had problems focusing. And blackouts at school for periods of time. Causing an unease in my behavior. My mind was in a still position and not on the school lesson. I left the classroom without notice. I had no responses to anything, drifting away with my mind. My teacher came down on me. He assumed no interest in learning so finally, he called my mother. My mother came to the school. I was afraid. There was a price to pay and trouble if mom came. Some mothers whipped their kids. I wanted no part of this.

Only if my teacher knew how much I cared, but my mind kept me back. He was so upset and wanted me punished. The teacher spoke with my mom and explained to her that I wasn't paying attention in class. She turned around and looked at me and went out the door. There were no beatings in the bathroom for me. When I got home, I explained to my mom. I had trouble understanding the work. My mom immediately said, "Get to the table so I can help you." I was relieved. I finished my homework and went to the closet with kitty. Only if they knew, my heart contained my tears. They're pouring in the inside. What should I do? My great grandma came sometimes. I had no relationship with a person of closeness. My thoughts were banging with negativity; nobody cares. I accept there's no change for me. I was in bondage (to restrain or confine), shackled to myself. If no one talked to me, I still had kitty; he was my companion.

This reminds me of a virtuous woman (exhibiting excellence, moral goodness) according to the Word of God. "Who can find a virtuous woman? for her price is far above rubies. The heart of her husband doth safely trust in her, so that he shall have no need of spoil. She will do him good and not evil all the days of her life" (Prov. 31:10–12 KJV). This woman of God, was my younger sister's grandma who would babysit us sometimes. She lived alone after her husband died. It was many years and she had no other companion, but she's fine with her life. When my mother needed a babysitter, she watched all the kids, not just her granddaughter. There's no separation with the kids. The motto was "if you do for one, you do for all." Everyone received something from her coloring books and puzzles. My grandma knitted and crocheted quilts, hats, and scarfs for everyone. In the building, we stayed on the third floor; she was on the first floor. There was a side window where she would holler upstairs early in the morning, "Kids, come downstairs and eat breakfast." Our breakfast would be oatmeal or grits, with a side of bacon or sausage.

God gave her more than enough for herself and others. Sometimes, we stayed with her in the evening. There were some black and white photos of her with family. She was beautiful with light blue eyes, wavy curly textured hair, and an hourglass figure. This remarkable woman spoke of the first automobile and airplane. The stories of her time were the best even the music (Nat King Cole). Her life was full of examples of right living and love for all. This was real love. Even at eighty plus, she never forgot our birthdays, and there were many of us. We received birthday cards with money each year. At her house, she would always welcome you with appetizers and desserts. When everyone left, it was her and I. She sat in her big chair. I would sit next to her on the floor and watch her knit. When I fell asleep, she would put me in bed and pull the blanket up. I knew of love.

2

Learning to Cope

My sisters and I attended a day care center in Chicago. I was around seven years old. There were programs for all ages—kids, teens, young adults, and adults. This place had tutors for homework, food pantry, thrift stores, housing, help for homeless, classes on life and living, recreation, and field trips. I remember there were celebrities like Oprah Winfrey and Mr. T from the *A-Team* inspiring others not to give up. Then Pope John Paul II, came to visit the nuns at the center. At around twelve years old, I engaged with the activities. The classes on life and living became my favorite ones. I could express myself in class and cope with my own issues. One day, there was a book discussed about a girl who had to cope with abuse from her own family. She had many obstacles searching for a better life, a courageous child, full of hope and from a tribe. This story touches the heart of many in the program. The child left home to start a new life and was under fifteen years old.

Whoever thought life puzzled many in this classroom. After hearing other people's stories, I realized that things could happen right under your nose or right in front of you, without recognition. Then sometimes, those who are aware said nothing, afraid to confront the situation not knowing what to do, or who to trust. Then unfortunately, the situation carries on, especially when it's a close relative like a father or uncle doing the abuse. Sometimes, the abused person is ashamed because they loved the person. Listening, I realized

I'm not alone. There was a girl raped by a relative and kids who lost their mom, the sister cared for them. The sister had no clue on how to raise kids; she was only a child herself. Just to hear others, it hurts, but those kids were surviving. This was a support group. Coming together, talking, listening and sharing our experiences helped me to release the weight I was carrying. Knowing that other kids had the same or similar situation. I spoke about mine with no shame. There was peace in my mind. The more I talked, the better I felt.

For some, if a person knows not the struggle, how can they relate? Some blame and accuse the victim to the point of shame, not knowing the position or the person's state of mind. For example, where they drugged, bondage? Not even taken this under consideration. Did the person come from a history of abuse? How's their mental capacity? "Let no corrupt communication proceed out of your mouth, but that which is good to use of edifying, that it may minister grace unto the hearers" (Eph. 4:29). The power of God's spoken word will change lives. Good lines of communication is important to be established, whether it's your children, wife, husband, coworker, or establishing a relationship. "Pleasant words are as an honeycomb, sweet to the soul, and health to the bones" (Prov. 16:24).

This center operated by nuns was a blessing in disguise. It was one of the best additions to the community. It gave you the opportunity to be yourself. I met other individuals who signed on to be a mentor. One lady from *Black Hair Magazine,* and the other was from a big corporation that she operated. The lady from *Black Hair Magazine* took me shopping for clothes. We went for a picnic. She laid out the blanket, we sat, and ate, then I went home. I never saw her again. At the other lady's house, which owns the corporation, I received a sweater. Her husband came and I had to leave, nothing said. I never saw her again. The nuns had no discussion of what happened to them. I understand committing yourself without knowing the facts or the responsibilities can change your mind about a situation.

Even then, I was still trying to figure it out. It appeared that something was pulling people away—those who wanted to help me. It was something not to pity me. I kept going, but unfortunately, this added on to disappointments and rejection in my life. Many people came and left—those who I cared about. It was just reality then, and I accept it. There was nothing I could do to change the circumstances. At least, the mentors accompanied me on the journey. There were other kids left behind. Which handled the dissappointment as well. They invited me to come along with another mentor, but I declined. I was really grateful that he asked, but I wanted the other person to have a relationship of their own with the mentor. Being around new people exploring different avenues. While at the day care center, the staff found work to do, and I helped. I prepared material for the next class, made snacks for the other kids and set the rooms for the visitors. Then I took part in other meetings and groups.

I immediately moved my mind and became helpful in other areas of the center, and this brought me great joy. Where I lived, it's possible everyone knew each other in the area. If something happened it was in every house. For example, an argument or fight, missing days at school and hanging out late. Nothing was a secret in the neighborhood. Is this the community outreach? Someone's family could expose you and look out for trouble. Were there televisions and cameras in every establishment plus on the streets. How did people recognize you or know your business? It is a strange situation. You knew nothing of them or where they came from. Some would say that the lady's kid on joy street started the confrontation that led to a fight. I could honestly say I didn't like this, but that on a kid's perspective.

Wherever it may be, everyone had a name on each block, door to door and house to house. Some people really had good intentions and tried to keep children safe by being involved in the community. Even then, some of this changed as time went on. A new generation arised. No longer were parents sticking together as much, There was no communication among them. Grown adults would jump in fights and beat up your kids, two adults would fight over the kids situations. For example, someone stole something from another child. Even in these situations, sometimes the kids are not always honest (maybe they lost it). Jealousy and envy became a problem. It was a time in school that teachers could intervene and possible stop an unpleasant situation from happening. But later, some teachers received no respect. I pray that our Heavenly Father brings up more leaders to minister the Word of God in every establishment and in every home and community, even on the streets. Amen! The lady from *Black Hair Magazine* changed my outlook. I saw different people, cultures and a variety of colors. Everyone was friendly, no one cared about your race. I'm grateful for every smile. Truth is, time is a blessing and an opportunity to gain. I had a fabulous trip full of excitement and adventure. There's always a place for wonderful memories.

Even though my mind remembered home but I had a time for peace. I hold the deepest part of me, I was smiling outside when I'm around others, but the inside of me told a different story. No one cared to notice the change in me. There were many signs to my behavior—isolated from people, problems at school, running away from home, and the list goes on and on. A lot of times, when you hear stories of child abuse, it's usually in the family or a friend of the family. Sometimes, it overlooked. Child abuse can manifest throughout your life and affect a person as an adult, having trust issues, unstable relationships and doubting love. I walk with my head down and I hardly gave eye contact to a person. It was difficult to address an issue. If called upon, my nerves went wild. People would say to me smile, but I was far from that.

"But whoso shall offend one of these little ones which believe in me. It were better for him that a millstone were hanged about his neck, and that he were drowned in the depth of the sea" (Matt. 18:6 KJV). I remember the story of Hannah (1 Sam. 1:20 KJV), "Wherefore it came to pass, when the time was come about after Hannah had conceived, that she bared a son, and called his name Samuel, saying because I have asked him of the Lord." Hannah went to the temple of the Lord and prayed and wept so for a child, and God answered her prayer. A child is a blessing from God! A miracle to cherish. I ask the question, have you told your child you love them? When was the last time? Are you saying this regularly? Building a relationship on love will keep you united. Showing love by action with kissing and hugging makes a connection. It's all remembered, even when times are rough there's a place for love. Especially for a child dealing with emotions. This can be a challenging battle. Taking you to a dark place than settling there according to the situation. If your communication, actions, and responses are in your feelings, they can cause a person's life to be chaotic and destructive. If a person doesn't see the underlining problem, this could cause more abuse.

My mom moved to a new location in Chicago. She enrolled us in the boys and girls' club, which was directly down the street from our house. I met new people; learn different sports like kickboxing, and how to do karate. Also, there were games and jump rope. The people would help with homework and give snacks. There were basketball tournments at the club with different areas in the community, mostly with boys. We attended another school that was challenging with the schoolwork. My mom kept us in some activities. Being on the street was no option and dangerous. She would search out a program. They sent us away to another city for camp by the nuns in the summer. As we were on the school bus, my mother stood there waving good-bye and crying tears. We were leaving for a week the first time. It was hard for her and challenging, but we had a great time. At home there were many stories and adventures (hiking, marshmallows at the camp fire, table games).

I was turning into a teenager. I started talking to two boys. One was sensitive, caring, and rough who could really fight. The other was laid-back and quiet. I talked to the laid-back one. He was so cute to me and could really play ball. Most of the time, we just talked and smiled. One day, I was at the club and the game was over. We walked down the street together. He stopped in his house for something, and I waited on him. He asked me to come in, so I did. I walked down the stairs, went straight, and then closed in. This space was very dark and small. I thought maybe a storage. This guy wanted to engage. If I decline, I would stay there, he said. This is unbelievable, I thought. I'm not sleeping with him. I couldn't see my hands in front of my face or my body. There was not a lot of movement. I was thinking, *What will I do?* I started to freeze; this was really happening. I needed help. I never thought this would happen to me. Conversations can deceive and looks.

I didn't go out crazy, but I was looking around and saw nothing. Then reality kicked in. The walls are closed in; there's no way out. When I think about this, I was afraid of the dark then. How was I able to block out the darkness from consuming me alone? I believe there was an interruption in my mind, and my thoughts stopped working. There was a void, a blackout. I was not there for many hours before the guy came back. I took some classes in fighting but few. I'm not a fist fighter, but a fighter to hold my feeling and emotions. When the guy opened the door immediately, my arms swung, and it was in a fight for my life. I was not the only one in that closet. Someone very tall, over six feet; solid built; wide chest, like a warrior from another life was walking me and swinging my arms perhaps in my body. This person had a lot of power, force, and might. I've never seen this before in the natural. That guy came down quick and laid out. No time wasting getting free, there was no thought of what happened or look back. I got out the door and ran.

I know it was not I who defeated this guy. There's no fight in me, I was running fast as I could and crying. I had no business there. What was I thinking? "Ye shall not fear them: For the Lord your God he shall fight for you" (Deut. 3:22 KJV). My friend's mother saw me while driving down the street. She picked me up. I was still crying. Asking what happened. I said a guy locked me in his house. He wanted to sleep with me. Tears flowed, like water from a faucet. I was so glad to see her, but afraid of her actions, we lived on the northside of Chicago. It was the grace of God that I made it out in one piece, and I had a ride home. I kept thinking in my mind, *What would my mother say? Would she go off into a rage?* My mom would always tell us to stick together. I knew my friend's mother would tell. When we arrived at my house, she walked to the door and knocked. My mom came to the door, and the conversation went on between the two.

I stood there looking. After the lady left, my mom closed the door. You could see the agony, she scolded me. Then she asked if I needed to go to the hospital. At this present time, I didn't care. I was mentally, physically, and emotionally gone. I started thinking of our relationship my mother and I—that I don't know her, and she doesn't know me. I've learned that spending time with your children is so important; it's remembered. No matter what, I still loved her even though I was unstable. I dismissed this guy from my life and saw him no more. The idea that this was becoming a pattern or a cycle of molestation or rape is too much. Another incident as a child when a friend came to the house. I was in the bedroom playing. He went to do something to me, and my mother saw this as she walked by. She freed me and said, "Run." I don't know if she hit him, but I ran. This guy was coming quick.

As I looked to the side, my mother was running with me. She fell and tripped over my feet, as if I ran too slow. At the day care center, I ran a lot of relays and I won. I could beat a person running who was older than I, but this day, I ran too slow. This is impossible and hard to believe. Running was a sport that challenged me. I'm competitive and could outrun older people. When this guy approaches, I'm immediately taken. I went up before I left the room. I could see what was happening. It appeared to be a robot or a figure in my place. That's why there was slow movement. It wasn't me. When I came back, I felt the disconnection between my mother and I like nothings happen. There was no conversation about this, but I knew she was upset and hurt. This was not my fight. Things changed between us. I felt no love. Later, I pack a jewel's bag of clothes to run away. I was thinking, *I didn't ask to come here.* I'm walking toward the stairs when she stopped me and said, "Get back in the house." Can you believe at that age I was walking out? How did I know to leave, I was a child? I was a quiet child who played by myself a lot. I started no fights or made trouble for myself. Unfortunately, trouble came to me.

The thought comes to mind, where's the father? I was outside playing, around seven years old. This lady came up to me whom I've never met. "I know who your father is." She said. This was his brother's wife. I looked at her and continued to play. Then later, I believe the same day. A guy came over to our house. I was told, "This is your father." It was strange, I looked at him and said nothing. This was the first time I met and saw him. This guy brought me a huffy bike and gave me $20. I thought he would come back but, he disappeared. I never saw him again at this time. For days after this, I watched out the window hoping he would return but that never happened. He called the house one day out of the blue. There were a lot of promises made but again no show. I didn't like this at all. My mother supported me by herself. I was his only child. I didn't understand why he showed up at all. If there was no intention of staying in my life, it's better not to cause any trauma. You've heard the old cliché, "Out of sight, out of mind." I had no thoughts of him until I saw him. Then, disappointment kicked in. I can't say my mother was the culprit in this because she allowed him to see me. For all that's done, I respect her highly for the opportunity with my father, even though it was unsuccessful. I still desired a relationship with him, and later in life I did.

3

Stepping Out without a Cause

I carried on with my life knowing nothing of patterns and cycles at around seventeen years old. I decided to leave home and stay with a girlfriend. There was strife between my mother and I (angry or bitter disagreement of issues, conflict). Instead of provoking each other, I left, believing this is the best. As I grew older, our relationship worsen. I didn't call or say anything. She had no idea of my whereabouts. I stayed in a toxic building unaware of activities which occur at night. Many drugs were being distributed and used. From crack, dope, marijuana, and happy stick. Whatever you need, it's accessible according to your desires. This was out of control. I wasn't exposed to drugs until then. Those who engaged were in their own world. To keep myself from screaming, I blocked the recreation out of my mind with no interest of drugs in any kind. There was no place for me. Where did I belong? I dealt with the situation and wanted to leave. The family crowded the apartment. It was like a motel, a place to use the water and change your clothes but not to stay and call home.

It was chaos there. People doing drugs in my face trying to entice me derailed themselves. There was a lady that abused drugs. I remembered from the neighborhood having a friendly personality, talking with people. Even at the center, no representation of her lifestyle she betrayed, you would say another person altogether. One day, she asked me to talk to her in the bathroom. I accompanied her with no questions to ask. You wouldn't believe a conversation helped interact the substance. If she stay focus on something else or being alert, the drug would not consume her dead. This is a load to drop an enormous responsibility, I was only a teen. When a person abuse drugs, do they want to die? that's not always the case. There's possibly an underlining condition causing a disturbance in the mind. The drug was occupying her mind from whatever reality that was troubling her. To really look at this, unconnected sources can control your mind at a time. I held the conversation to control the mind. She directs her response towards me keeping the mind functioning. The third party, the drug, was the overall mind control that consumed the focus and gave the feelings or emotions.

The drug I believe was more desired. It weakened the body plus it was alive. A manifestation took place, to see this was terrible. I didn't want her to die but feeling obliged to help. Her eyes rolled back in her head, only seeing white. I thought she slipped away, you could see the drug take effect. Her body slumping down to waste. She was falling into a sleep standing up losing mobility, then a shift took place. I heard her speak. She was alive. I asked myself while writing this, where was your mind? My mind is on the battlefield, while living in the natural. The Word of God says in Ephesians, "For we wrestle not against flesh and blood but against principalities, against powers, against the rulers of darkness of this world, against spiritual wickedness in high places" (Eph. 6:12 KJV). First Peter 1:13 (AMP) says, "So prepare your minds for action, be completely sober [in spirit—steadfast, self-disciplined, spiritually and morally alert], fix your hope completely on the grace [of God] that is coming to you when Jesus Christ is revealed."

How important is the mind in what you perceive (become aware or conscious of, come to realize)? I believe it changes your emotions, feelings, and understanding on a situation. It upholds all responses, actions, and movements. According to how well it's kept determines your progress. Your mind is key as to the heart. If your mind is unstable then your thinking is your focus. As you speak to those at times, there's a picture painted of yourself, and in some cases, you're judged by it. I've heard in my life to think before you talk and also before a conscious decision. I recall as a child having my share of Budweiser beer by different babysitters. They believed that beer puts a child to sleep. I know it worked, and I slept. According to KidsHealth, alcohol is a depressant that slows down or depresses the brain. Like many drugs, alcohol changes a person's ability to think, speak, and see things as they really are. How could I function in myself? My thinking was interrupted. I remember tempting to jump off one building to another as a child. Being under the age of ten years old. We were running outside and playing. I was next to the youngest. The other kids were around fifteen years old. One climbed onto the roof, so we all did.

While on one roof, the other kids jumped to another roof of a building. They all made it safely across. When my turn came, I looked down. I saw the long drop, but I jumped anyway. I ran fast and stretched my legs for a leap, and dropped. There was a force pulling me down from somewhere. It was a hard quick tug or pull racing. At this moment, you would say good-bye, but God said no. As I was being lifted and carried across. I came back to myself when I landed on the other side. Taken again by surprise. Glory be to God. Hallelujah! There was a war going on for my life. Something wanted me to die, and God wanted me to live. Thank God for mercy and grace. Where I lived, certain people pressured me to do drugs. Being called all kinds of names. Some said, "You're not better than anybody." You think you're all that. I did not engage, not even a cigarette or dope. Drugs were popular commodities there, but I had no desire for it. I continued on with school and dealt with my housing situation.

My mother's house was not an option for me. I was a middle child. Some older kids gained because of the age difference. The younger received an abundance, being the last child. What about the middle child? Have you ever given them leftovers or hand-me-downs and thought it was okay? Or tell them you'll give theirs later. Big mistake. The older I got, the more I separated myself. Caring for only those who cared for me. There's to much hurt and pain in me. I could not shed a tear. I came to visit another friend of mine who stayed with an older man. Their apartment was a small studio. The bed was out in the opening, and I sat on it. We talked and laughed. I could forget myself for a while, but feeling hungry, I asked for food. At this point, I would take anything. She gave me a bologna sandwich and Kool-Aid. Something happened unbelievable. I woke up with two other girls, not knowing how many hours I slept. But it was dark outside and light when I got there. How could this be? I don't take naps nor was I tired after eating.

I checked my clothes and the other girls. My pants were on. I knew them, but I still felt violated. Did someone touch me? One girl went to the refrigerator and pulled out the pitcher of Kool-Aid. The red Kool-Aid was foggy and cloudy. This reminds me of preparing the charcoal for a barbecue. After the fire is out, the charcoal's smoke is white, and it rises. As I looked on the Kool-Aid, you could see the pill substance floating around. I believe set up. The old friend checked the Kool-Aid right away. There were several pills missing from the guy's medication. There was a garlic crusher sitting on the counter, this was probably used to crush the pills and a job to do. That's a big pitcher. You could tell there were issues of drugs before this time, because they checked him first. The girls were displaced needing somewhere to stay being puzzled by the situation. Drugged without notion, for what cause? Death in no case consume me. Thanks be to God! The blood of our Lord and Savior Jesus Christ.

4

Who Could I Trust?

There was a change in my life. I dated guys again. I met a guy on my way home one day. He had a big smile, he was about six feet two to six feet four in height and two hundred plus pounds, mostly muscles. I believe no fat on the body, built like Arnold Schwarzenegger and older than I. He came around the apartment building alot. Sometimes, I spoke with him and other times, I didn't. There's no rush to go out. Not trusting many. To persuade or convinced me was the ticket. This guy's appearance was neat and clean, well groomed. He was fair skinned with long, curly, textured hair and a charmer.

Speaking educated, with a wide span of vocabulary and meanings. This guy's hands and nails were clean and white. On hot days, he wore sandals. You could tell pedicure, from the nail shop. His toenails were white, along with his teeth and pink gums. He cared about his maintenance and conducted himself like charm school (a school or course in which they teach polite manners and proper etiquette, grace and social skills). He enticed with gifts, expensive jewelry, and clothes. I thought kind and generous, but I didn't believe in taking gifts. This was no option for me. Our conversations would be detailed and interesting about life and experience.

One day, I went to a Mexican restaurant with him. He was just a gentleman, opening doors. Even pulling out your chair and seating you. He was an icon or a model (to some of importance, wanting to be like or symbol). People watched him. There was not a hair out of place. This guy likes to order your food. Both of us had tacos with everything and a Coke or Pepsi. While the food was being prepared, he went to the restroom. I sat in my seat and waited. I started to feel uncomfortable at the hard stares, like someone's watching me. When the guy returned, he sat down no conversation and ready to eat. There were two Mexican guys on the grill cooking. I knew without a doubt they were watching us. When I looked up from my plate unexpectedly, their heads turned. I thought because he was older than I, or they knew him. The look was uncommon to others. It's amazing how they stared but never said a word kept staring. I continued to watch them fear was on their faces. After lunch, we left the restaurant and went to the car. I sat in the front seat of the car looking dazed. My reactions were slow, and my focus was off. The longer I sat, the more something rushed me.

I was fighting in myself to remain, but I went out. Woke up at a prison. How did I get here? I looked around and fell out again. How could this happen? I'm thinking about this now. At the restaurant, he went to the restroom before the food came. There was no food on the plate. I had no food or drink in his absence until he came back. I was so busy focusing on the guy I came with, even though I was suspicious and uncomfortable. What about my surroundings.? Sometimes, there are other people involved as well. He spoke nothing of a favorite restaurant, but he knew the location of the restroom.

A small area hidden in the back corner. You would mistake it for something else unless you were there before. While eating, the guys on the grill watched anxiously for a reaction to the food. Their faces had a look of desperation (sign of desperation—being overly interested), ex. Waiting on a phone call or a first date. How could this be? Where's the love for people? I thought at that time. They drugged my food for him. That this all was a conspiracy, and the cooks knew this guy. That they were the setups. Maybe getting paid for their participation. I woke up the next time in prison, being paraded around men (paraded—walk or march, display (someone) publicly in order to impress or attract attention).

This guy was advertising my body with clothes on. In a stand still position being held up. I had no control over my body. I couldn't feel myself. Can you imagine? Putting a person to bed that's more asleep than awaken. That was unaware; they fell asleep. What's happening to me? I'm thinking of that afterschool program on channel 7. The date-rape drug, according to Healthline, was used to make a person vulnerable to sexual assault and easier to attack. Sometimes, one or more drugs are used to distract a person, so they become unaware of what's going on and unable to protect themselves. These drugs are often secretly slipped into someone's drink. When a date-rape drug begins to cause symptoms and how long they last depend on how much you're given and whether it's mixed with alcohol or other drugs. Alcohol can make the effects even stronger. Symptoms of date-rape drugs generally include dizziness, confusion, and loss of memory. The resulting loss of inhibition (inhibition, a feeling that makes one self-conscious and unable to act in a relaxed and natural way), impaired judgment, and memory loss are reasons why these drugs are used in rap.

They are sometimes called "paralyzing" since the person often loses muscle control and is unable to move or call for help. The most well-known date-rape drugs include Rohypnol (flunitrazepam), which is prescribed to people with sleep and anxiety disorders in some countries but not approved for medical use in the United States. GHB or gamma-hydroxybutyric acid is sometimes prescribed to treat narcolepsy (a condition characterized by an extreme tendency to fall asleep whenever in relaxing surroundings). GHB is also called cherry meth, liquid E, ecstasy or scoop. Another drug was ketamine, which was used during surgical procedures. It may be called vitamin K, Cat Valium, Kit Kat, or Special K.

I have to accept the fact that this is reality. Medication is not always used in the best interest of others. (Mercy God!) At this moment, I'm thinking, how did this guy get access to these drugs? Did he know someone or date the doctor, or bought a prescription? And used people for pawns. I hear the term ghetto boy, hood boy or deadbeat, but I've seen people with major careers date them, love them, and marry them. (For example, doctors, lawyers, teachers, etc.;

all kinds of ethnic backgrounds are included, not one in particular.) After the prison, I fell out again and woke up in a large three-flat building. This building was off white or beige. The construction was old stone bricks. This was a masonry construction. The building's location was low-key in a back corner next to a chicken shack in the city. I was still focusing my eyes from being intoxicated.

I could see this guy through a mask or covering over my face. He was engaging himself. I was on a bed. Even then, the body was dead weight. He was trying to position it. I had no response, only a blank look. I felt nothing. There was no care in the world, just raping me, he thought. He left the room. I came out this form of a body and sat straight up. My head was not pounding. I looked all around the room I just got there. Where am I? Then immediately, I put on my shoes. I asked myself, how could you lift yourself straight up, not lean to the side for support? Being intoxicated with drugs? I immediately bent down and tied my shoes without hesitation. The drugs never rushed to my head as I bent over. I got up and went straight for the door. When I opened the door, there was a fog of white smoke. This place was very cloudy. The apartment was enormous with so many people. There were drugs in the air. A lot of pipe smoking, crack, cocaine, and marijuana; people of all ages and different nationality. There were those who walked past and stared with little to nothing on, like lingerie. I heard no music playing. This was not a party but a hang out. As if those drugged themselves before work.

I saw many women but few guys. There was a woman who stared extremely hard. Reminds me of the movie *Blade*. In the movie, vampires came at Westley Snipes trying to kill him. The look on their faces was demonized (possessed), another kind and form. Same with this woman. She came, staring and studying me as if she wanted to attack. Then looking back as she walked by. I looked desperately for the door. I thought this woman would alarm others. There were people looking, but no one stopped me. I found the door leading out. On my way out, I noticed how long the hallway was in this apartment. There were so many people here. It was unbelievable, even in the back of the apartment. I went out the door. There were a lot of stairs, and it was a long way down. Reminds me of a long tunnel with stucco on a dry wall. I held on to the wall and walked down the stairs. There was so much weight on me. I was heavy to walk down the stairs but only weighing under 140 pounds (weight: pressure, burden, as the weight of grief, weight of care). I made it out the front door, knowing where I was. This was a busy area.

There was a grocery store that conducted a lot of businesses. The chicken in the box place was loaded with customers. The prostitutes walked up and down the street soliciting customers. This area was the hot spot. I was not myself, staggering from the confusion in my mind of what just happened to me. Staring at the people outside as they watched and stared at me. Being judged as a prostitute. As I continued to walk down the street, cars slowly passed by with their windows hanging out. They were just watching. No one helped. The look I had was of a teenager. It appeared to be a conspiracy in this area. There were a lot of houses with many watching on every corner. I was trying not to cause attention to myself but slipped away. How could I? I wanted to run. Who would come after me? I recall riding past this area seeing prostitutes soliciting up and down the street with little to nothing on stopping cars. This was a pickup and drop off area for them. What was I to do? I was an acceptable distance from the place and going along. Then a car pulled up quick to the curb on my right side. The guy from the restaurant that wanted to sell me. He jumped out of the car wanting to use force. There's no doubt or confusion about it, I was not there. But up in the air, and someone was holding me up as before.

I believe there were others protecting as well. It was like floating but not moving out of place in the air. I was out and came to looking down in the natural while still in the air. Basically, only the outside covering of my body was in the natural to see. The inside was in the air. I could see what was happening to my body in the natural. The guy ran up swung and hit me. He was beating my body with a blow of fists. Then he began kicking me especially in my back, as if he was kicking a ball for a field goal at a soccer game as I walked down the street. This guy's shoe size approximately a thirteen. He went mostly at my head with both hands, rolled tightly in a ball, and pounded at the top middle of my head. You could tell he's had much experience with this. He gave me an image of a wrestler, like the old-school World Class Championship Wrestling. These wrestlers would pound on each other while staggering until someone loses consciousness. This guy was trying to immerse the drugs in me to have an effect or kill me if not. I would have no recognition of thinking and no life. If I live possible, he could control me under the influence.

Somehow, this guy believed I was still myself. There was no controlling me with the drugs, so he wanted me to die. I knew his appearance. How could he beat my body and kick me, wherein my bones would break in half? I said no words or scream. Being only a size five in clothes, very thin, five feet five in height. Not stumbling or falling. I stood straight and kept walking through this entire ordeal. There was no way I could live through this. If that guy hits me one time in the natural, I was dead. I'm not in denial. I believe the truth. "The Angel of the Lord encamped round about them that fear him, and delivereth them" (Ps. 34:7 KJV). He didn't hurt me, I had no broken bones, and there was no blood; and this was on a major street in Chicago. Mercy. Thank you, Jesus! Hallelujah! God Almighty lives! "But Jesus beheld them, and said unto them, With men this is impossible, but with God all things are possible" (Matt. 19:26 KJV). I say it again, the way he performed was like a wrestler. As if he had some kind of special training. His face at that time was in disfigurement. It was another face and his. The look was of a killer; he was so angry and violent. As if I did something personally to him or his family to cause the rage. It was so much trauma.

I couldn't believe this was the same person. He was a monster. There was only so much he could do without a disguise. Unless he wanted to end his life or be on the run. So many people were watching, so he left me. I made it back home and told no one. It looked like nothing happenned. I learned from a guy later that he was a pimp. I've watched a lot of old movies, and he had no resemblance of a pimp. He wasn't flashy. He wore a leather sports jacket and jeans. That was average and plain, but he had long hair. There was jewelry on his neck but not as visible, and he offered me some. I looked for the gold ring on the pinky finger, kangol hat, and maybe a fur coat. The talk (taken care of you) I consider those to be pimps and players. It hurts being tricked and deceived. There was a guy who came around the neighborhood every now and then.

Looking at me with interest. He said nothing to me then. But one day, he did. I was told the pimp, along with the leader of a notorious group, had a bet on me. The bet was the pimp could prostitute me by a certain time to receive a substantial amount of money. The leader of the group believed this was impossible to do but not the pimp believing he could prostitute anyone on the street. He was so determined and invincible to himself. The pimp wanted the money badly; I had no idea of the amount. The race was on. When this news came to me, he was running out of time and also getting reckless looking for me. Thank God! Someone told me the plan. I had to fight back or die trying. I ran every time I thought I saw him, for the chase was on. Then one day, I was on my way home walking down the street. This pimp pulled up behind me in an unfamiliar car. He got out the car and went to grab me from behind. Can you believe I asked no one for help, not even the police?

There was another guy in the car whom I've never seen before. I was thinking at this time to fight hard. I heard these pimps took the girls to another area from home and prostituted them. In this City and other places. The pimp tried to put me in the car. It was an old car. I was holding on to the car. One hand on the front door handle passenger side, the other hand on the back of the car. The pimp kept looking back. Watching for bystanders or witnesses as he tried to abduct me. I was holding on like a cat fighting against the water. Glued to the car. To get me in the back of the car was not my plan. He was pushing with force. Getting frustrated. The words coming from him, "This is crazy, get in the car." There was no way, after beating me up and down the street, that I would get in this car. The other guy in the car turned around. It's amazing he was ready to pull off with me. Thank God! He didn't get out of the car to help him. There was no way I could hold on to a car like that. It was like my fingers became claws, stuck in something. He finally gave up, and I got away again. It seemed like I was out of trouble. He left me alone for a while.

Then one day, I was at a corner store on a major street. There were many people outside. I saw him. My first thought was, no way he could touch me with all the people watching. But my heart dropped. I started rushing. First down a major street, then I took shortcuts down a side street. I believe he missed me. I felt relieved at this time, but I started running. I couldn't believe this was happening to me again. How sick is this situation? This pimp had no care in his heart for people. His whole aspect was money by any means. I was running for my life. A few feet from a relative's house when the pimp pulled up. It was rapid. I was so afraid. His car was half in the street and half by the curb, for he left the car in hot pursuit of me.

I was at the door of my relative's house, knocking hard. It was a reckless situation and no one came. This time, my heart was racing and aching with pain. Fear corrupted my understanding as he approached me. There were no words to say. Then a car pulled up. It was my mother with a male friend. She got out of the car, came toward me, and said, "Who is this guy?" I said nothing and rushed to my mom's vehicle. The pimp went back to his car and pulled off. I was in shock, but I was glad that someone saved me. I didn't look back, and I never saw him again. "What would have happened to us? If the Lord had not been on our side. When people attacked us, they would have swallowed us alive when their anger flared against us: (Ps. 124:2–3 NIV). Thank you, God.

I went home with my mother but only for a short while. We had nothing in common. She knew nothing of my life. I left home again. This time, I stayed with relatives and worked a job. I was gone for periods of time. When one relative robbed me, I could not comprehend this. My relatives knew I had nothing to give them. Some didn't care. I had nothing to take and starting from scratch. One relative tried to take my clothes off while I slept. He was pulling my pants so hard that he woke me up. It was so awkward, looking at him and catching him in the act. He was lying on the side of me in my bed. When did he get there? How could he do this? I needed help even to talk. Trouble was all around. Mercy on me!

I needed my father! I've heard of our Lord and Savior Jesus Christ, God our Father, but my memory was not present. I continued in my own way of living. No matter how good I was, those would try to use me for anything. I was constantly told I was too nice throughout my life. I've learned that this is a crime to some and an opportunity for those to take advantage or abuse. Knowing throughout my life Jesus saved me. I was right next to stray bullets that missed me by inches in a nightclub. I was out with a girlfriend. Someone started shooting in the party. All the people scattered. It appeared that the bullets were very close. I told my friend to run, and she stood in shock. I shook her. Then she took off running. We both stayed under a table.

Then another time, I was over a friend's house. We were all outside on the front when someone pulled up and started shooting. All went to run for the front door. The gun sounded like a 360. I was the last one running. I went for the door, and they locked it. I dropped down on my knees between the front screen door and the house door. Staying there; the shooter kept shooting into the front door. I was still on my knees turning the knob to get in the house while the shooter kept sending rounds of bullets into the house. I never got in the house. Sometimes, you see on television how the shooters get out of the car with the guns and come toward the house shooting. This never happened. Thank God! The screen door was not strong or sturdy. It was not metal. The shooter finally stopped and left. They never saw me in between the screen and the front door. Can you believe I'm still here to tell the story? Glory be to God! As thoughts come to my mind, I remember working at a known grocery store. I was a cashier. There was an older gentleman who came to my line. He was causing a scene. He kept saying, "I know it's you. I can tell from the gap in your teeth it's you." I've never seen this man before. I said to him, "Let me ring you up, so you can leave my line." Thinking this guy is crazy. He finally left my line after causing a scene.

Then the store closed, and the police came charging in. There were many of them outside and inside. It was like the show cheaters on television. I couldn't believe they were looking for me, but yes, they were. Can you believe they took me off my job, like a criminal, no questions asked? They handcuffed me in front of everybody. It was like *America's Most Wanted Criminal.* I was so embarrassed. This was unbelievable. They put me in the squad car with a hand on top of my head. They took me to the police station. Being put in a white room and interrogated, handcuffed to a chair. I was in a rage. I had no wrap-sheet. I've never committed a crime in my life. There were no fingerprints on file for me. It's one word against another, but I did no wrong.

What was the charges? Who said I did something? How could they charge me without evidence? There was a guy waiting outside. I asked the police to allow the guy to come in and look at me. He's making a mistake. The police finally allowed it after much begging and pleading. The guy finally came in the white room. He looked in my face and said that I was the one. I was being harassed by all parties, even the officers without knowing what I did. I thought this is not right. Finally, I was told that myself and a girlfriend came over his house. I had to stop him from lying. I told him, "No way would I go to your house. I don't sleep with old men." He left the room for drinks. There was a large some money in a shirt pocket.

When he came back with the drinks, the money disappeared and he never saw us again. I was in a state of shock and denial. It was not until a person came in and told me my rights that I believed. I was thinking this is a joke, but I've heard the rights being told enough on television to know it's real. What's happening? I had no criminal background. They took me downstairs in the police station and fingerprinted me against my will and they put me in a cell by myself. Look at me! I was condemned without a cause, turned around, looked at this small space and had no reaction. The toilet was black, and they connected a bed to the wall by a chain (the bed was a thin mat). It was like a dungeon (underground prison). Not long after being locked up, someone came, took me out of the cell then to an office. The chief superintendent at the Chicago police station looked at me and said, "Let her go." (Thank you, God!) He didn't believe it was me. For this cause, I know there's innocent people in prison and to pray for them, for this happened to me.

"And the Lord said, I have surely seen the affliction of my people which are in Egypt, and have heard their cry by reason of their taskmasters, for I know there sorrow" (Exod. 3:7 KJV). "Behold, I am the Lord, The God of all flesh, is there anything too hard for me?" (Jer. 32:27 KJV). "Many are the afflictions of the righteous, but the Lord delivereth him out of them all" (Ps. 34:19). I couldn't see myself going to that job again so I left that job and found another. I left the house of my relatives and found myself an apartment. Things were looking up. Then one day, I was off work. I went to the grocery store. Then I came home. I walked in the house, went toward the kitchen; the back door was open. I immediately started looking around for something. I believe there was not enough time for them to steal. I came home too quick. Someone was watching me, I believe. I was only at this apartment for one week. Even at this time, I had no memory of my past, and if I was still under attack. I called a relative to drive a truck, and I moved out again. I moved on the other side of town; new surroundings, different people. I had to get away from the old. This apartment was beautiful. I loved the paint job, and no one in the area knew me. I was happy again. I came home from work every day. My things were still there, I thought. Then I got up one morning, looking for a certain item.

I noticed that they were missing. As days went on, it was becoming a regular habit. Something was missing. Until one day, I quit! I went to my reality company and gave them the keys. I believe it was an inside job I called the movers again. Moving again, I found another apartment. Each apartment was better than the first. I had an upstairs and a downstairs, one bedroom and two bathrooms. At this time, I only had a few articles to take or pack. There were few clothes or shoes but I kept going anyway. Focusing on trying to live. I came home one day. I took my coat off the day before and placed it on the chair. It was missing. The lock on the door was still in one piece. How could this be? I was only there for one week. Knowing, I was being watched even more. I marched right to the manager and gave the keys to the apartment. I had to leave again, but something strange happened this time. The manager told me, "I don't know if you believe in God, but the devil is after you." How is this? This was only the second time I spoke with this manager. She knows nothing about me or my life. I chose not to respond to this. I'm just looking at her. I knew in my heart that there was something going on. How could this lady know, unless she was told? Truth is, she was right and I believed her.

Someone shed some light. Thank God! There's no way bad things kept happening. I wasn't a bad person, but some thought I was because of my life and circumstances. I don't know if it involved the pimp, but the average would think so. It was something to maintain myself. There was a lot being said about my character. That I was throwing my life away. I loved the streets. I needed to get my life together. Fact still remains. I never asked for any help, and some of my own disrespected me. Everyone in my family wasn't bad, but I choose not to come around as much at all. The less they knew about me, the better. No one would know my business. Sometimes, you get comfortable around certain family members and tell your own business while holding a conversation. Even then, there's a price to pay for most if your family are gossipers. It's amazing how sometimes you don't see yourself or the position, just the status of other people. Also, for those outside looking in could only see an image but not what's contained. "Thou hypocrite first cast out the beam out of thine own eyes; and then shalt thou see clearly to cast out the mote out of thy brother's eyes" (Matt. 7:5 KJV). "Let all the bitterness and wrath and anger and clamor and evil speaking, be put away from you with all malice: And be ye kind one to another tenderhearted, forgiving one another, even as God for Christ's sake hath forgiven you." (Eph. 4:31–32 KJV). "For if ye forgive men their trespasses your heavenly Father will also forgive you" (Matt. 6:14 KJV).

One day, I took a bus ride out of the area. I rode all the way to the end of the line, longer than two hours. I got off this bus and looked around. It was a quiet area. I walked down the street and decided to cross. There were two cars sitting by the curb parked with no driver present in either. There were no oncoming cars or traffic. I stepped in the street, in between the two parked cars. I was looking straight ahead. The car that was in front started coming back toward me. I had no idea. I thought no one was in the car because I looked before I went on the street. She kept coming back, and I fell down on the ground and almost completely under her car. There was a lady in another car screaming. How could she back up without looking in the mirror? There were no cars in front of her. The only thing to do was wait for the green light and go straight, but she came back toward me for no reason. I was almost flattened, but somehow, I pulled my body and dragged it to the sidewalk. I laid there. Thank God!

The lady who hit me got out of the car, stood over me, and said, "Did I want her to call the police?" She had a cell phone in her hand, pretending to call. She was wearing a black sheer scarf tied under her chin, round big black sunglasses, like a disguise. She appeared to be Hispanic. The car she drove was an old antique. I believed the lady that was screaming and hollering called the police. The driver fled the scene, and they took me to the hospital by the ambulance. I was examined. Nothing was broken so I went home. How could trouble find me. I've had my share of accidents. I remember getting hit from behind while sitting still at a red light on three different occasions. Each time, I was sitting there waiting on the light to turn green when my car was rear-ended by one or more cars. I remember one time it was a chain reaction. Every car involved collided into the next. I went right into the steering wheel. My car was hit so hard that in one case, they twisted the trunk of the car into the back wheel on the passenger side. Then another time, my car turned circles quickly in the middle of a big intersection. I just froze. There was nothing I could do.

I couldn't scream, and my mind went blank. I was in a state of shock. How could I be alive? There were many cars coming on both sides of the intersection. I've never seen this before, but the cars stopped on both sides of the intersection and allowed my car to finish spinning, as if someone told them something or stopped them all. Then another time, one of my girlfriends had an old Buick sedan around 1980. I was on the passenger side when a Chevy van, around 1988, hit the car and came plunging through the driver's side into the car. The driver jumped on my side, and I was balled up in a knot. Also, one day, I was getting on the expressway making a curved turn, and I knew my car was still turning but more on the edge to nothing. I could feel my car being pushed back on the road. Glory be to God! How my life looked to some, I had to be doing something wrong.

How did I get here? I didn't ask for trouble, but somehow, it came. It's still a continued cycle of occurences. Some would say, "Why me? Am I being punished?"

I always had a heart for people, but it wasn't always the same for me. As a child, at the day care center operated by nuns, we visited people in the nursing homes. I was around twelve years old. The people were sad and crying. You could feel the tension in this place. Sickness was running rapid all over the facility. There was not enough care for the people and a shortage of love. Some had no family members left. Then others just had no visitors at all. The nuns bought many gifts for the people. They gave us the opportunity to pass them out. I saw some smiles from the people. That would touch your heart. It felt good to give. That's something. I would never change about myself. There was a break in the frustration. No matter what happened before at that moment, there was a release. Good-bye to sadness! There was a new day and a new atmosphere.

Then another time, I was seven years old, when an apartment on the third floor was on fire. I was on the first floor with my grandmother. No one else was in the building. My grandmother was about seventy plus years old. I thought we would run out the building. Instead, she grabbed her pocketbook, which was her purse and other articles while I was in despair. I wanted to say, "Let's go," but I was a child. I was watching her go back and forth. I wanted to leave but not without her. Even though I was in a panic, I waited patiently. I loved her. I wanted nothing to happen to her. She took care of me, and I had to take care of her. "A new commandment I give unto you, that ye love one another; as I have loved you, that ye also love one another" (John 13:34 KJV). Glory be to God! As a young adult, I was still pressing on, even though the setbacks were getting the best of me. The more I thought (meditate) about my life and the disappointments, mistakes, and regrets. I couldn't bare it that I laid in bed and cried. I wanted to die so I prayed it. At this point, I felt defeated. Look at me!

5

A Cry for Help

At this time, there was nothing I could do. I was at the end of my rope. Even my body was drained, weak, and dehydrated. Is my life leaving me? Depression and oppression consumed me; my attitude began to change. There was an anger and uproar with me. I battled with the reality of where I was in my life. I'm getting up there with numbers. How stable am I? I thought to leave the city. I knew some who packed up with kids and left that city with nothing and as a single parent. To hear the accomplishments with housing and a job excites me with so many thoughts going in my mind. I had no control over it. The more I laid in self-pity (excessive, self-absorbed unhappiness over one's own troubles), I was killing myself and every part of my body. I needed help, and who would help me? For those saw me and the struggle. Even though I didn't talk of all things, somethings couldn't be hidden. Like the house being robbed continually and the car accidents. As I look at it, pride played a role in my life without the recognition of it (pride, an unreasonable conceit of one's own superiority in talents, beauty wealth, accomplishments, rank or elevation in office).

The aftermath was killing me to want to die (How could I move on? When I don't completely understand). I had to get over myself and people. Who cares what they think? (I'm creating the problem right here!) If I changed the way I think—my emotions, responses, and actions—then I would be free to live without shackles and negativity. Then nothing else would matter or what it looks like (I could walk by faith). I needed a change! (How could I not see myself?) That I thought for people, and came with my own responses for them and then judged their actions toward me on what I perceived of their thinking. Sometimes, the people never had to talk. I just knew, I thought. (There was a recording playing in my mind, and I meditated on it.) Then I blocked myself from asking for help. Some battles or struggles were beyond my control. I needed help and I was drowning in myself. I gave in to stress and worrying. It became a part of my normal activity until my head from the pressure hurt.

How long will I suffer myself to myself? For as long as I allowed my (flesh) to be in control of my life (flesh: a carnal state; a state of unrenewed nature). "For all have sinned and come short of the glory of God" (Rom. 3:23 KJV). I had to recognize no one's perfect. There's no way I could fix myself by myself. I didn't have it all together or know the answers. I needed guidance, a stable foundation, a solid structure that's unshakeable. For quitting was not an option even if I want to something says no! Mercy on me, God! How can I explain this feeling not knowing myself or who I am. Still, I cry!

Then one day, I was leaving the apartment where I live, I met this guy. This person was different with words and conversation (he was peculiar, you had to read in between the lines). After several run-ins and conversations with him, he asked me to come to church. It's like something registered in my mind—church. I remember you Lord! Then later on, I found out the guy was a preacher.

> And he spake this parable unto them, saying, What man of you, having an hundred sheep, if he lose one of them, doth not leave the ninety and nine in the wilderness, and go after that which is lost, until he find it? And when he hath found it, he layeth it on his shoulders, rejoicing. And when he cometh home, he calleth together his friends and neighbours, saying unto them, Rejoice with me; for I have found my sheep which was lost. (Luke 15:3–6 KJV)

I ran for the church. I needed the path of righteousness. Nobody knows me like the Father. He doesn't care what I look like.

When I think about what happen with myself and church, it's sad to say. I left church because of me. I was my own problem. My heart was not clean. I was concerned about other people—their thoughts or reactions—when my thoughts were not right. Why did I think about people's thoughts or reactions in the church? I brought emotions and feelings of the past. When those people don't know me, if they never met me or been around me. I caused some of my own issues. (A part of me was missing.) My focus was on the wrong thing. It should be God the Father; the Son Jesus Christ, our Lord and Savior; and the Holy Spirit; and learning to live according to the Word of God. The Bible—our instructions and the way we should go. Church is the place to hear the Word of God and apply it to your life. It's inspiration and inspiring to one's soul. I tried God; I went to God just as I am and surrender my life to God. I repent for my sins (to change the mind, or conversion from sin to God). "Repent ye therefore, and be converted, that your sins may be blotted out, when the times of refreshing shall come from the presence of the lord" (Acts 3:19 KJV). "Then Peter said unto them, Repent, and be baptized every one of you in the name of Jesus Christ for the remissions of sins, and ye shall receive the gift of the Holy Ghost" (Acts 2:38 KJV). I accept the Lord Jesus Christ as my savior. I believe he died for my sins. "That if thou shall confess with thy mouth the Lord Jesus, and shall believe in thine heart that God hath raised him from the dead, thou shall be saved" (Rom. 10:9 KJV). I can't go on being a victim of circumstances or blaming others for my life. The more I hear the Word of God, the more I desired to change in my heart.

There is an answer for me and a way out. The name is Jesus Christ. I had to commit myself. I know in my heart I needed a new path and a new direction. As I continued to hear the Word of God, There's a need of fresh baptism. This time around, I was seeking more. I needed the manifestation of the Holy Spirt to be present in my life. I needed guidance. "And I will pray the Father, and he shall give you another Comforter, that he may abide with you forever" (John 14:16 KJV). "But the Comforter, which is the holy Ghost, whom the Father will send in my name, he shall teach you all things, and bring all things to your remembrance, whatsoever I have said unto you" (John 14:26 KJV). (The Holy Ghost or Holy Spirit, the Divine Spirit; the third person in the Trinity—the Father, and the Son, and the Holy Spirit—the sanctifier of souls, the Holy Spirit; sanctifier: to make holy, set apart as sacred; consecrated). I picture Jesus coming out of the water with an abundance of light. The glory upon him. The heavens opening. The Father acknowledging his son. For this is marvelous in all the earth. (John the Baptist desired to be baptized by Jesus, but Jesus wanted baptism from John the Baptist. "And Jesus answering said unto him, Suffer it to be so now: for thus it becometh us to fulfil all righteousness. Then he suffered him" (Matt. 3:15 KJV).

I saw an Apostolic Church on TV and right after the people came down the aisle and gave their life to God. They dressed them in a white robe with a white cap on their heads. This was the first time that I saw people being baptized during the service. No appointments needed. I knew to run and find this church immediately. I found the church in Chicago. Apostolic Church of God. The service was so inspiring. It began with prayer. This was no ordinary prayer. It was for all people and the nation. For the sick, shut out and bereaved. For we all need the love of the true and living God. Next was the praise and worship. The whole church praised God with dance, song and musical instruments. Then the Word of God came from the anointed one. It's amazing that God really knows you, and I mean everything! (Your favorite color, your desires, what you need, what you're doing, and what you've done. God knows!) God was talking to me. You know, when you hear all your business, there's no denying the truth, it's you being spoken to!) I was so ready for a change in my life. It was almost time for the minister to say come. Then it happened. The man of God said, "Come." I didn't care what I looked like or who was watching. I got up and walked down the aisle. I was smiling so hard, and joy rushed me like a flood. What took me so long? (I did.)

Someone welcomed me and touched me, and took my hand, then another and another all the way. Then I reached the area of baptism. I changed into my white, like what I saw on television. Then someone met me again. My hand was taken, and I walked to the water. This was the best thing I've ever done. I was so excited. The light guided me, and my expectations were high. I stepped in the water and stood still. As the minister spoke the Word of God over my life, I agreed and accepted the Lord Jesus Christ as my savior. Then I was immersed in water, taken away, rushed and over showered. I came up seeing rays of light in different directions. My mind was in glory. Brightness, luster, splendor, magnificence. It was so white. There was no person in sight at this time. I was pressing hard to see clearly. Being overwhelmed. It was a task keeping me on my feet. I was not the same. This was a fresh experience. It's amazing. When I was baptized before, a different experience, but this time, the lights blinded me. After baptism everyone went to a room.

We were told to read Acts 2:1–4 and to keep saying, "Thank you, Jesus!" As we repeated the words, "Thank you, Jesus," there was another voice that spoke out of our mouths, a different sound of another language.

> And when the day of Pentecost was fully come, they were all with one accord in one place. And suddenly their came a sound from heaven as of a rushing mighty wind and it filled all the house where they were sitting. And there appeared unto them cloven tongues like as of fire, and it sat upon each of them. And they were all filled with the Holy Ghost, and began to speak with other tongues, as the spirit gave them utterance. (Acts 2:1–4 KJV)

> And I will pray the Father, and he shall give you another comforter, that he may abide with you forever. (John 14:16 KJV)

> But the Comforter, which is the Holy Ghost, whom the Father will send in my name, He shall

teach you all things, and bring all things to your remembrance, whatsoever I have said unto you. (John 14:26 KJV)

This was only the beginning of my walk. I still needed deliverance (deliverance: to free; to release, as from the restraint to set at liberty).

After this manner therefore pray ye: Our Father which art in heaven, hallowed be thy name. Thy kingdom come; thy will be done in earth as it is in heaven. Give us this day our daily bread. And forgive us our debts, as we forgive our debtors. And lead us not into temptation, but deliver us from evil: For thine is the kingdom, and the power, and the glory, for ever. Amen. (Matt. 6:9–13 KJV)

I've learned that deliverance is not an overnight process. "I sought the Lord, and he heard me, and delivered me from all my fears" (Ps. 34:4 KJV). "Then they cried unto the Lord in their trouble, (and) he delivered them out of their distresses" (Ps. 107:6 KJV).

It's amazing how God supplies all your needs. I went to work one day, and a lady who worked in another department came in the office and talked frequently on several occasions about church. She invited me to her church, and I attended. The church was an Apostolic Deliverance Church. It was a unique atmosphere and so intense. People were really serious about praising and worshipping God, and I mean overwhemingly. After hearing the Word of God, taking effect on my brain, mind and thinking, and heart. I was in acceptance. The anointed apostle of God asked if any one needed deliverance to come down the aisle.

I was in need to release those things troubling me. For example, molestation, rape, self-affliction, depression, hurt, disappointment, rejection and fear. Some things happen that I had no control over, especially as a child, but I carried the weight of every situation and ever encounter. I needed freedom in my heart, brain, mind, and thinking (deliverance). I had to forgive myself and others for me. Let the pass go or never be free to live without shackles. For example, wanting love, need attention, wounded, acceptable to any type of behavior, feelings and emotions are running your life, having the wrong reactions and responses, then accuse and blame, pass judgment on people, trust issues, complain, finding something wrong. My God, help me, Jesus! I know, Jesus, you're a heart fixer and a mind regulator. Mercy on me! I couldn't get ahead; the past keeps bringing me back. For example, what people did to me, or how they treated me; it was me me, me…I'm the pity party whose going through this and troubled? just me. Whatever they did, it's done. They don't care. I realize I'm my own problem that for every unpleasant situation that happened in my life or disappointment, it stayed in my heart. My heart was contaminated.

When I reached the altar at the church, they assigned me an altar worker. God began to minister through the woman to me, talking of different situation that arose in my life. I knew it was real. The women of God knows nothing about me. She didn't ask me to tell her something first about myself in order to get a response from me. You would say your business was pouring out of her mouth through Our Lord and Savior Jesus Christ. I cried harder than ever to my knees until I bowed down as a fragile piece of material nothing. There's a lot more to deliverance. One thing for sure, no one knows you like God the Father, the Son Jesus, and the Holy Spirit the Comforter. "For if ye forgive men there tresspasses, your heavenly father will also forgive you: But if ye forgive not men there tresspasses, neither will your father forgive your tresspasses" (Matt. 6:14–15 KJV). "But I say unto you Love your enemies, bless them that curse you, do good to them that hate you and pray for them which despitefully use you, and persecute you" (Matt. 5:44 KJV). Through it all, our Lord and savior Jesus Christ remembers all. The bottom line, I had to forgive myself and others. This was difficult alone. I needed help from our Lord to continue my deliverance.

I had to ask for deliverance wholeheartedly, believing that I can be free from my past. I don't have to stay in bondage. God can help you and I, by myself, can only make it worst. No pride, or arrogance. Receive wholeheartedly. Say yes to his plans, his purposes for your life. Open your heart, know that it is your portion. "But upon Mount Zion shall be deliverance and there shall be holiness; and the house of Jacob shall possess there possessions" (Obad. 1:17 KJV). "For the Lord God is a sun and shield: The Lord will give grace and glory: no good thing will he withhold from them that walk uprightly" (Ps. 84:11 KJV). Be submissive to the Word of God (to be a doer to the Word of God, ready to change and conform). Surrender to the will of God (be obedient). Come in compliance; you've done it your way for so long. Try God! Hear the Voice of the Lord, listen for direction through the Holy Spirit to live and save your life. He desires none to perish. There was something that's controlling my soul that causes me to submit to my flesh and the will of others. For example, it's like wanting to eat something knowing you were told it will make you sick, but you have it anyway.

The Book of Genesis 3 states:

> But of the fruit of the tree, which is in the midst of the garden, God hath said, Ye shall not eat of it, neither shall ye touch it, lest ye die. And when the women saw that the tree was good for food, and that it was pleasant to the eyes, and a tree to be desired to make one wise, she took of the fruit thereof, and did eat and gave also unto her husband with her; and he did eat. (Gen. 3:3,6 KJV)

Even though Eve knows what God said—eating from the wrong tree would cause death—she allowed herself to be enticed and influenced; she still ate. The mind (heart) is powerful with many avenues, compartments, and connections. It has to be guarded with your life! I had to get free. I kept coming to the church for deliverance. The more I received deliverance, the better I felt. I had to learn who I am in Christ Jesus. "So God created man in his own image, in the image of God created he him; male and female created he them" (Gen. 1:27 KJV). "For ye are all children of God by faith in Christ Jesus" (Gal. 3:26). "Therefore If any man be in Christ, he is a new creature: old things are passed away; behold, all things are become new" (2 Cor. 5:17 KJV). "I am the vine ye are the branches: He that abide in me and I in him, the same bringeth forth much fruit: for without me ye can do nothing" (John 15:5 KJV).

As I think about the Word of God touching my life, I'm reminded of the story of Moses. Because of fear of the Hebrews being many and strong, so Pharaoh gave this command to his own people. If the Hebrew women give birth to a baby girl, let it live. But if they have a baby boy, you must throw it into the Nile River. (Exod. 1:22, Biblegateway, easy read; The birth of Moses Exodus 2:1–6 Biblegateway, easy read). Moses's mother hid him for as long as she could, after three months. She made a basket and covered it with tar so that it would float. Then she put the baby in the basket and put the basket in the river in the tall grass. Pharaoh's daughter went to the river to bathe. She saw the basket in the tall grass. Her servants got the basket. Pharaoh's daughter opened the basket and saw a baby boy. Pharaoh's daughter knew this was a Hebrew baby. Even with Moses's mother, when you love someone, it's hard to walk away! Moses's mother gives up her child. She made provisions for her son.

Moses was beautiful to her. She protected and covered him, He had an opportunity to live. Even though she had to leave, but was not forgotten, she still provided. Moses had to experience life without his natural mother sometimes. He had trials and tribulations. But through it all Moses became a great man of God whom the Lord used to do signs and wonders unto Pharaoh and the Egyptians in order to free his people. Read Exodus KSV chp 7. Our Lord and savior Jesus Christ make the provisions. He gives the way out. Sometimes we can focus on the problem and create more obstacles for ourselves then were fighting to get free. In life you will have challenges but there's a lesson to learn through every situation that will carry you to the next level in your life. If you don't give up or quit pray and ask our Father the Lord and savior Jesus Christ for his will in your life and not your own. You can't go forward looking back. Keep your head lifted. Have faith and believe He knows what's best for you Jeremiah 29:11 NIV says. For I know the plans I have for you declares the Lord, plans to prosper you and not to harm you plans to give you hope and a future. That's a praise to God! Hallelujah! I am not a victim! So I choose to forgive and love again! For God's grace and mercy endures forever and is sufficient enough! To God be the Glory. Amen! As for this time in my life, I continue to study and educate myself in the Word of God and inspire through my gifts and talents that our Father has bestowed on me through writing. While I yet still breathe and able, there's opportunity for change. For as I continue to seek God for guidance, he gives avenues of his plans and purpose for my life. There's no failure in God Amen!

John 1:32 (MSG)

I watched the spirit, like a dove flying down out
of the sky, making himself at home in him.

About the Author

After this manner therefore pray ye: Our Father which art in heaven, Hallowed be thy name. Thy kingdom come, Thy will be done in earth, as it is in heaven. Give us this day our daily bread. And forgive us our debts, as we forgive our debtors. And lead us not into temptation, but deliver us from evil: For thine is the kingdom, and the power, and the glory, for ever. Amen. (Matt. 6:9–13)

Lalita Walker, inspired by the Holy Spirit, continues to acquire knowledge being educated as a servant, sharing the good news of the gospel. She prays that in sharing her real life events that lives will be changed, setting people free from themselves, allowing the Spirit of God to work in their lives, and capturing their hearts and receive salvation, setting a new path for a fulfilled life.